WEDDING MUSIC
FOR CLASSICAL PLAYERS

To access companion recorded piano accompaniments online, visit:
www.halleonard.com/mylibrary

Enter Code
3225-3167-1182-3358

ISBN: 978-1-5400-2042-0

HAL•LEONARD®

Visit Hal Leonard Online at
www.halleonard.com

Contact Us:
Hal Leonard
7777 West Bluemound Road
Milwaukee, WI 53213
Email: info@halleonard.com

In Europe contact:
Hal Leonard Europe Limited
42 Wigmore Street
Marylebone, London, W1U 2RN
Email: info@halleonardeurope.com

In Australia contact:
Hal Leonard Australia Pty. Ltd.
4 Lentara Court
Cheltenham, Victoria, 3192 Australia
Email: info@halleonard.com.au

Depending on the situation, sometimes wedding service music must be abbreviated or expanded. Feel free to find optional cuts, endings, or repeated sections as needed.

CONTENTS

JOHANN SEBASTIAN BACH

4   Air from Orchestral Suite No. 3[1]

6   Arioso (Sinfonia)[2]

8   Jesu, joy of man's desiring[2]

LUIGI BOCCHERINI

12   Minuet[1]

CHARLES GOUNOD

16   Ave Maria, adapted from Prelude in C Major by J.S. Bach[1]

GEORGE FRIDERIC HANDEL

20   Hornpipe from *Water Music*[1]

24   La Réjouissance from *Music for the Royal Fireworks*[1]

26   Largo from *Serse*[2]

GUSTAV HOLST

28   Jupiter Chorale from *The Planets*[2]

FELIX MENDELSSOHN

30   Wedding March from *A Midsummer Night's Dream*[2]

JOHANN PACHELBEL

37   Canon[1]

ERIK SATIE

40   Gymnopédie No. 1[2]

FRANZ SCHUBERT

42   Ave Maria[1]

GOTTFRIED HEINRICH STÖLZEL

46   Bist du bei mir[2]

RICHARD WAGNER

34   Bridal Chorus from *Lohengrin*[1]

Pianists on the recordings: [1]Brendan Fox, [2]Richard Walters

The price of this publication includes access to companion recorded piano accompaniments online,

for download or streaming, using the unique code found on the title page.

Visit www.halleonard.com/mylibrary and enter the access code.

Air
from Orchestral Suite No. 3 in D Major, BWV 1068

Johann Sebastian Bach
Transcribed by Celeste Avery

Arioso
(Sinfonia)
from Cantata, BWV 156

Johann Sebastian Bach
Transcribed by Celeste Avery

Jesu, joy of man's desiring

from Cantata, BWV 147

Johann Sebastian Bach
Transcribed by Celeste Avery

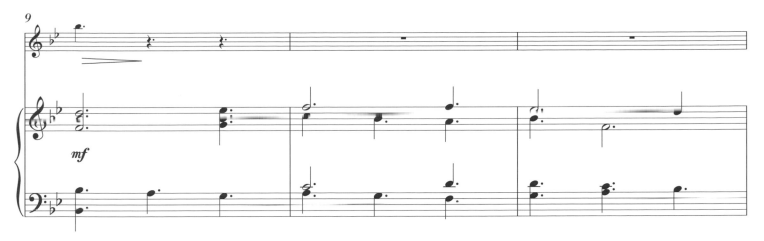

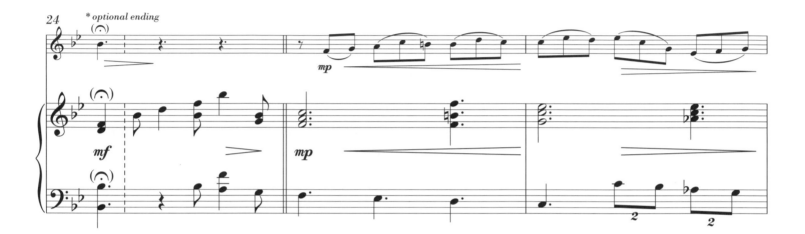

* fermata for optional ending only

Minuet
from String Quintet in E Major, Op. 11, No. 5

Luigi Boccherini
Transcribed by Celeste Avery

Ave Maria
adapted from Prelude in C Major, BWV 846 by Johann Sebastian Bach

Charles Gounod
Transcribed by Celeste Avery

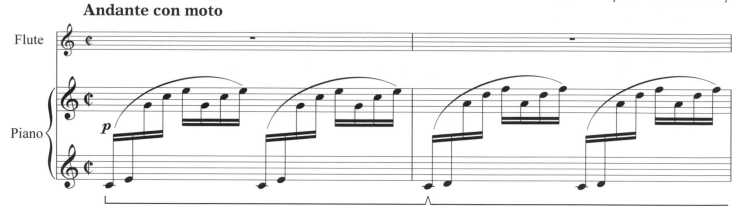

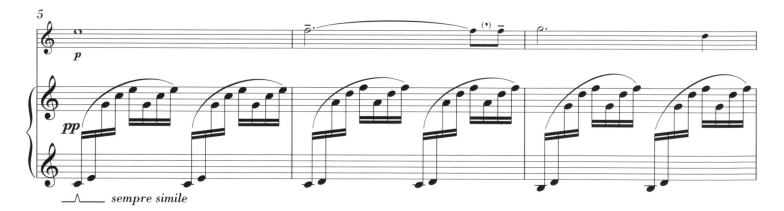

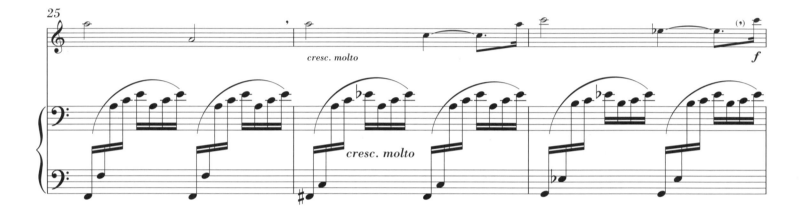

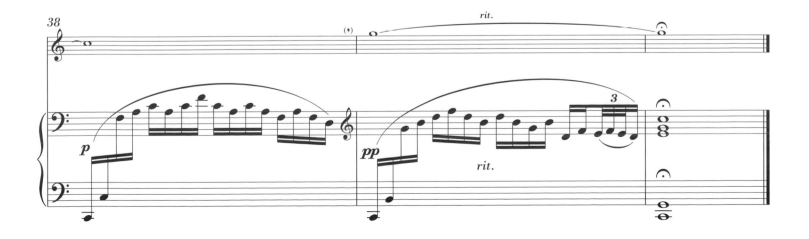

Hornpipe
from *Water Music*, HWV 348

George Frideric Handel
Transcribed by Celeste Avery

La Réjouissance
from *Music for the Royal Fireworks*, HWV 351

George Frideric Handel
Transcribed by Celeste Avery

Largo
(Ombra mai fù)
from *Serse*, HWV 40

George Frideric Handel
Transcribed by Celeste Avery

Jupiter Chorale

from *The Planets*

Gustav Holst
Transcribed by Celeste Avery

Wedding March
from *A Midsummer Night's Dream*, Op. 61

Felix Mendelssohn
Transcribed by Celeste Avery

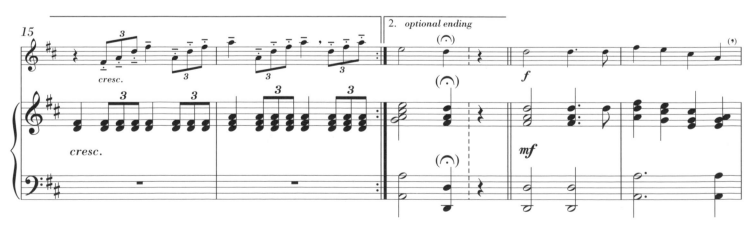

Bridal Chorus
from *Lohengrin*

Richard Wagner
Transcribed by Celeste Avery

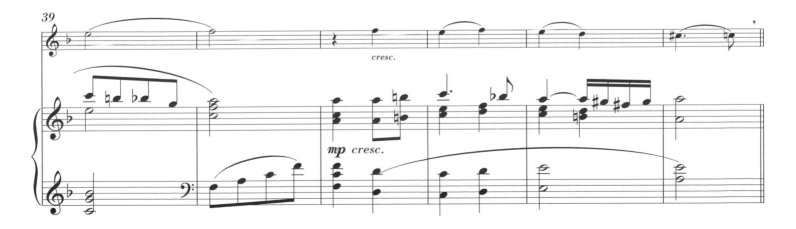

* For a shorter version, begin here after four measures of introduction.

Canon
(Canon in D)

Johann Pachelbel
Transcribed by Celeste Avery

Gymnopédie No. 1
from *Trois Gymnopédies*

Erik Satie
Transcribed by Celeste Avery

Lent et douloureux

For a shorter performance, the piece may begin at measure 40.

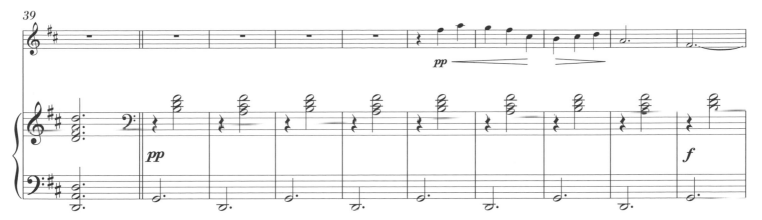

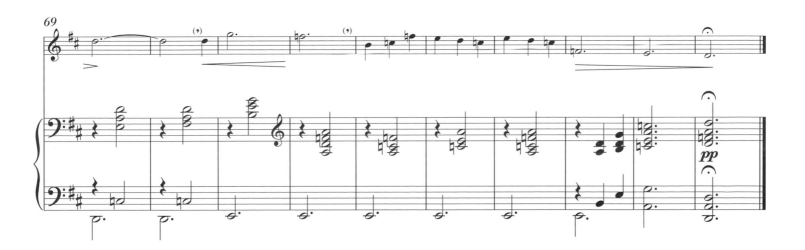

Ave Maria

Franz Schubert
Transcribed by Celeste Avery

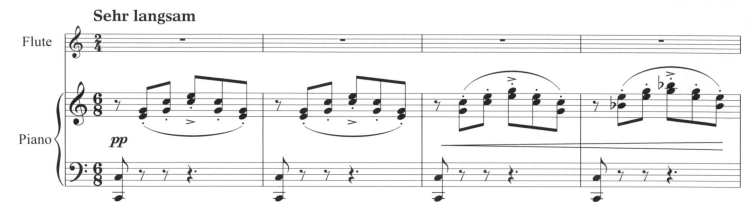

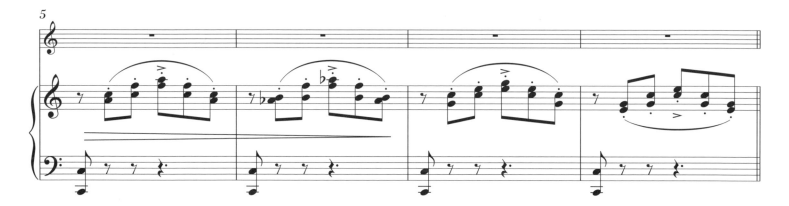

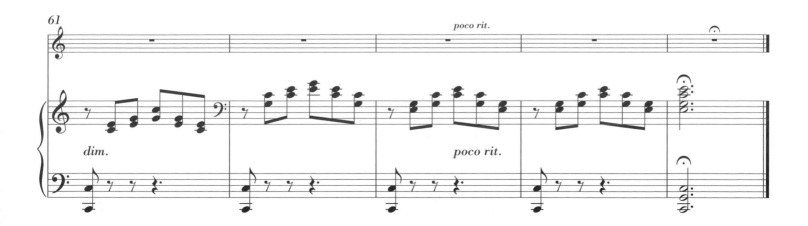

Bist du bei mir
(You Are with Me)

Gottfried Heinrich Stölzel
Transcribed by Celeste Avery

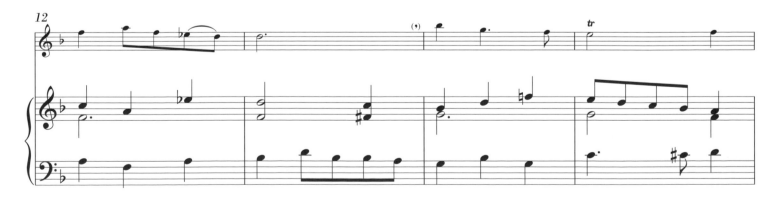

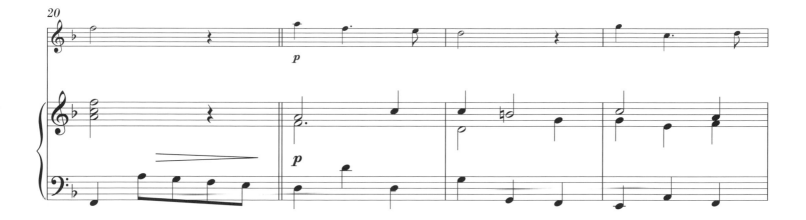